T0128278

DESPONDENCE

NATANYA HAYLES

WESTBOW
PRESS®
A DIVISION OF THOMAS NELSON
& ZONDERVAN

WestBow Press books may be ordered through booksellers or by contacting:

WestBow Press
A Division of Thomas Nelson & Zondervan
1663 Liberty Drive
Bloomington, IN 47403
www.westbowpress.com
844-714-3454

Interior Image Credit: Natanya Hayles

ISBN: 978-1-6642-0630-4 (sc)
ISBN: 978-1-6642-0629-8 (e)

Library of Congress Control Number: 2020918311

Print information available on the last page.

WestBow Press rev. date: 11/10/2020

This book is dedicated to my benevolent mother, who was my number 1 supporter in the creation of this piece. You consistently encouraged me to write more, even on my dark days. I love you so much.

This book is also dedicated to my past self, to my past lovers and my past friendships. Thank you for being a vehicle of transformation in my life. Through these interpersonal and intrapersonal relationships, I have been able to measure my growth and Lord knows that I have grown so much.

Thank you, God, for blessing me with the ability to be highly intuitive and sensitive. I couldn't have grounded myself and sat down and write, if you were not such a powerful presence in my life. I love you.

CONTENTS

YOUNG, WILD, AND DUMB

Into the ashes, into the dark

I make my mark on the young impressionable girls before me

If I documented every day of my life in my teenage years, I would play it for you

so that you stay clear of the road that I walked on

It would save you a lot of tears, and hopelessness and doubt

but, if you're like me, I know that you want to experience it for yourself

so, when you need to cry, I'll be there to hold your hand

and tell you that you're okay

and you will be okay

I'M HERE FOR YOU, LOVE

My heart weeps for my sisters and brothers going through pain

To have your dignity stripped away by another person considered your equal is..

heartbreaking to say the least

Speak to me and squeeze my hand

I'll do my best to comfort you in your pain

I couldn't fathom the dark road that you had to lay your head on

I couldn't grasp the eerie shadows that you had to fight through in order to see the light

But, I am here

in whatever capacity that you want me to be

I want you to promise me that you will be kind to yourself

on this journey of self-healing

Even if there are days you feel like the world outside your room is too scary to encounter

I want you to know that you're making progress

Don't neglect yourself

Step away from your phone

Breathe in the crisp outdoor air

Stretch your back into the horizon

Soothe yourself to the comfort of hot ginger and lemon

You will be okay

The universe loves you

LONELINESS

I get so lonely sometimes.

Especially after 12am, I feel Loneliness creep into my throat and sink down to my stomach, making himself at home.

It's a familiar feeling for me; Loneliness is no stranger to my body.

He comes and goes, as the seasons' changes, as the day turns into night.

He's always there, hiding in my subconscious.

Even when I had a good day with good company, I think to myself, "Loneliness must of vent on vacation, he left the door unlocked."

And then hours later, he comes back.

He doesn't need a key, Loneliness will always have access to my home.

He's a maddening tenant that I can't get rid of. I can't get rid of him.

Do you know how many times that I've tried to get rid of him?

I cry and I scream and I shout, "Loneliness please leave me alone! I don't need you in my life! Please go!"

But, he doesn't listen to me.

He's immune to my cries, he doesn't care.

He's immune to my cries, he's always there.

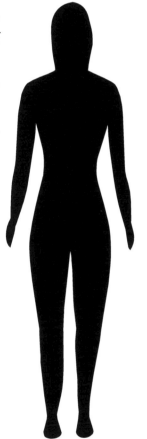

3

LONELINESS IS FRIENDS WITH INSECURITY

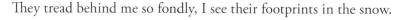

Loneliness is friends with Insecurity.

They laugh at me when I have no one to talk to.

They laugh at me when my sister and I fight.

They laugh at me when my mother and I fight.

They laugh at me when I am trying hard to quiet my sobs.

They follow me around, noticeably during the winter months.

They tread behind me so fondly, I see their footprints in the snow.

They keep me up at night and whisper nasty things in my ear.

I try not to believe them.

But, it's so hard to resist them.

The only pastime they know is taunting me.

I CAN'T TALK RIGHT NOW

Please close the door on your way out

and don't come back

Please leave me alone for the day

...for the week

...for a month

I don't have the energy anymore to converse

Emotionally and mentally, I am drained

I notice the people around me are drained too

I'm not the only person going through something

But, let me wallow in my suffering for as long as I want to,

even if it exceeds the amount that I *need* to

I'll leave this state eventually

Presently though, my thoughts are cloudy

My room is a mess. I'm not groomed

I'm not the only person going through something

But, please let me cry for as long as I want to,

even if it exceeds the amount that I *need* to

I don't want to die anymore, which is good

I just want to sleep

I just want to be alone

I don't want to talk to anyone

I'm sorry. I'm trying

I'm not the only person going through something

But please let me isolate myself for as long as I want to,

even if it exceeds the amount that I *need* to

SUBDUED TO SORROWS

Depression will migrate you through different stages.

At first, you'll cry.

Your tears will stream down your face, unto your lap.

Your mother will come into your room, eager to talk to you, after a long day of work.

You'll snap at her, insisting that you need space.

She'll notice your tears and will ask you what's wrong.

But, you have no energy to explain.

She'll then leave your room, dejected by your sadness.

You also won't be able to eat.

For three days, you'll go without eating before you pay attention to your stomach's whimper.

Your bones will feel weak, and your body will become lethargic.

You will feel like a prisoner to your own bed, engrossed by the filth you created in your room.

After a week, you will feel better again.

You'll smile with your mom. You'll speak to your sister again.

You'll get up to make eggs for breakfast.

The darkness will soon return; however, engulfing your vision.

You won't take care of your hygiene.

You'll go a week without showering.

Your hair is dirty and dry.

Your skin is riddled with acne.

You don't want to leave your house.

You'll stop talking to your friends.

You'll curl up in your bed, and drown out the noises from the outside.

Depression has won this battle,

and he is laughing.

UNTITLED

I miss you,

and I wish my tears were not falling down my face for you.

As I lay in my bed, watching the sun set from my window,

I can't help but miss you.

Soon these mild tears will turn into a lump in my throat,

and I would want to ball.

But for now,

I'm reminiscing about,

the time we spent together.

Our connection was intrinsic.

I felt that,

you were my soulmate.

I miss you,

and I wish you weren't so cruel.

You were my favourite.

I miss you.

1 SIDED BATTLE

I look in the mirror with bewilderment.

Some days I feel so proud to look at myself.

Other days I look at my face with disgust.

I don't wish to battle with my physical appearance.

I receive enough external validation to believe that I am in fact worthy.

That I am deserving of good things.

In this world, if you're appeasing to the eye, you will receive good things.

I struggle to see what other people see when I am looking at myself.

It's hard for me to admit that I do not like myself, on days when the void in my body becomes too overpowering to ignore.

I can scratch at my imperfections until I bleed out

but, it won't soothe the pain.

For me to be at peace with myself, I must accept myself

and for me to accept myself, I must find love internally.

I BLAME MYSELF

My eyes burn when they well up with tears

I shouldn't be crying, I don't deserve to feel sad

I wish you were here to comfort me

I miss your warmth

and I hate myself for becoming codependent again

but, it's so easy to fall back into routine

I can't fall asleep, if you're not there to hold me at night

I can't get out of bed, if you're not the one I wake up to

Why did you choose to love me, when I am a mess?

why did I choose to love you, when I am a mess?

I NEED TO LET YOU GO.
I MUST LET YOU GO.

I left you in the shadows of a dark forest

to go to a stream to fetch for water.

I found life in the bountiful stream

and the water replenished me.

I'm so grateful that I left you behind in the shadows

because when I was with you, I felt my life source depleting.

My light was escaping me.

I gave you all of my light

and you gave me nothing.

KILLING ME SOFTLY

I love you but,

you are draining my energy.

I can't see you every day,

and I can't feed your sexual appetite any longer.

There's more to life than staying in bed with you.

Please stop living in your romanticized world.

You're suffocating me.

I REGRET THIS DECISION

I can't let myself down any longer,

and the things that I did in the past haunt me so much, that I'm finding it hard to forgive myself,

and it's no one's fault but my own

No one will carry the burden, but me

I know what I have done, and I dread the outcome

If I could die right now, I would feel relief

For my actions are so foolish, I cannot fathom that it came from me

My thoughts are all cloudy, and my energy is low

I can only be mad at myself,

I reap what I sow

OVER IT

I'm still thinking about you, and it hurts my heart that you ignored me.

I don't really care.

Yeah, I don't really care.

TAMIRAH

I don't know why you make me so mad.

I wish I never entered this territory.

I didn't know the grey area would be so dangerous.

I lost my best-friend and I lost him.

But, I never had him to begin with.

I thought I could.

The friendship between you and I was already fading.

I'm angry.

I'm angry.

I'm so angry.

It's really myself again.

Not saying this to garner pity.

But, it's really myself again.

I'm sorry to the people who send me love letters and get no reply.

I don't want you.

I want misery. I want despair. I want tears

It seems like.

NO LOVE

I'm not finding love in these people.

There's no love in these people.

There's no joy in these people.

There's no home in these people.

There's no peace in these people.

OCTOBER, 2019

Give me any reason to romanticize us, and I'll be dreaming for days.

It's better that I don't let you into my space

because every time I close my eyes, I see your face,

and the memories of you and I, our fingers entwined and our lips pressed together is hard to erase.

I try to speak to you, but I struggle with finding what to say.

I wrote you a text and deleted it like 5 times.

You said that you will call me but it's after 9, and you still haven't hit my line.

The thought of being undesirable brings some insecurities in me.

Even though there's many chasing me, you're the only one I seek.

I need closeness. I need trust.

I need consistency. I don't need lust.

I need a hand to hold and skin to skin contact.

Without it being confusing. I need a call back.

I know you want me to open up but what for?

So, that you can take my softness and my vulnerability and walk through the door?

When I try to say what I really want to say, my words are rooted in fear.

I just want to start brand new, but these negative feelings are drawing near.

It's like I always repeat the same cycle. I'm always in the same situation.

It's like the only way I learn is through trauma and desperation.

What I'm trying to say to you is, I like you, and I want us to be close.

Can we take it a step back? So, we can share secrets nobody else knows?

Let's start out as friends and

see if this journey will end.

THIS ONE IS FOR ME

Seeking kindness in you is ridiculous of me to do

You're not even kind to yourself

You only feel important when others validate you

External factors will satisfy you for a short while

When the euphoria subsides, you will feel hollow again

Until you learn that joy and love come from within

STAY THE SAME

In a world that's constantly changing, why do you remain the same
and why do you stay complaining?

You lay in your bed too long that it becomes your prison

Lingering in your sorrow won't allow you to complete your mission

and running away when it gets too hard won't allow you to grow

Didn't your mother tell you that you reap what you sow?

So, every day you repeat the same patterns and remain in your melancholy because that is all you know

In order for you to fly, you need to open your mind to the sweetness of life

You are an abundance of love and light, yet your self-defeat refuses you to shine

When you realize the power that you carry, life will become so sublime

MYSELF

I constantly go through changes

Right now, I experience more lows than highs

because when I go through it, I stay in it for a while

I am learning how to pull myself out of depressive thoughts

and I am learning how to fight my battles without the need to escape

In my eyes, I am my own hero

I wear the cape

ANGEL

An angel came to my doorstep at 3:33

to tell me that everything will be okay.

As long as I commit to my personal growth, I will find my way.

When I stop to face my challenges and feelings of discomfort

that is when I know I am soaring.

There will be times when I feel like I am lost or helpless

and there will be times where I feel defeated.

But, I comfort myself by knowing that I am on my path to freedom.

My angel reassured me that my thoughts are true

and it will take some time to outgrow the patterns which I knew.

I cried in her shoulder and she held my face.

She told me that I am indeed on my way

to a life of abundance, wealth and beautiful bouquets.

She hugged me tightly before she left

and before she left, she said that I should not let self-doubt inside of my head.

I agreed and watched her disappear

into the atmosphere, into the air.

I cried some more, and I still felt her presence.

She gave me the tools to enter a new transcendence.

I moved forward with love and with light

finding solace in knowing that my future is bright.

I HATE HIM NOW

When you lean in to kiss me, it's the sweetest thing.

Your lips are so gentle, and your eyes are kind.

You place your hands firmly on the back of my neck.

I feel blood rushing to my cheeks, and my heart-rate accelerates.

When you hug me, I feel a surge of euphoria pulsate through my body.

You are my calm, and you are my comfort.

ENAMORED

Maybe I can admit that I want to be praised

I want to be adored by a lover who isn't my lover

I want to be the object of your desire

I like when you stare at me

I know that you are utterly enamored by me

I know you're in lust with me

The twinkle in your eyes burn brightly

And I love it when you squeeze my inner thighs

But I know this connection will not live long

I can feel my energy draining when I am beside you

You're no good for me

I'M BLUE

sometimes I wish I had a person to tell me goodnight

to look me in my eyes and tell me everything will be alright

to hug me, to love me

to take my breath away

even when I am upset or moody, that person will stay

I want to be held

I want someone's intimacy

I know that I can be a complex person, riddled in intricacy

because sometimes I want my space and I am heavily guarded

but for the most part, my heart is open, yearning to be softened

NEVER WILL I SEE YOU

Be gentle with me

Be kind to me

Don't lie to me

Don't hide from me

I know you see the wall I keep

that divides you from me

My wall is high

My worries are multiplied

I'm too anxious to say what's on my mind

So, I sit and I cry

and I watch you say goodbye

There was no room for our love to grow

My heart was kept in shackles, my words could not flow

The connection between us was fleeting

So, now you feel defeated

I promise you cannot come back to me

For that, I am free

VOID

got out of bed today

the escapism has made its way back to me

numbing out my body to coexist with my responsibilities has always been the path I walked on

but, I'm not in too deep

I can get off this path

I will get off this path

the hard part is making my legs agree

my energy is leaking from my body like a broken faucet

I'm withering away steadily and my petals are falling off

waking up at 7 am turned to 8am then it turned to 10am then it turned to 2pm

the void repetitively opens and closes within me

THERE'S A SPACE BETWEEN US

I put you in charge this time.

I know you won't meet my expectations.

I know you'll forget about our plans.

Something in me just wants an excuse to talk to you.

I just want you to reply.

FINE-LINES

Take the one-night stand away.

Take the inadequacy away.

Give me friendship, support, consistency, sincerity, laughter.

Help me reach my potential through platonic means.

I can't afford to get lost again.

I can't afford to let myself down again.

HARD TO ADMIT

I took a walk to clear my mind

but, still sitting on top of my head

was your silhouette

You looked so good when I last saw you

I wish my mind could produce a physical picture

so, I could look at you all the time

We would look so good together

but you hesitate to acknowledge me

I wish you weren't so busy,

but you vowed to put yourself first,

and I should do the same.

C'MON GIRL

He didn't text you back yet

but, were you expecting depth?

You knew what his intentions were from the start,

and now your stomach is sinking to the ground and your heart is beating fast and you remember how he treated his last girl and you wish that was you.

You're so predictable.

Longing for something that you will never get.

You sought safety in the lesser attractive; they were humble.

But, you got bored and flirted with the devil, only for your body to be thrown into the fire.

It's pointless

because you knew this was going to happen.

But, you fight with yourself,

and you ignore your own voice

and you doubt that feeling in your stomach that screams when danger is near.

Now that feeling has turned into a tight knot deep in your abdomen.

Honey,

this boy is not for you.

As pretty as he is, and as tall as he is and as soft-spoken as he is.

He is not for you.

He still hasn't texted you back,

and if you coil yourself up into despair

and refuse to unravel until he pays you any mind...

you will be coiled forever.

You already lost when you were upset that you could not find your validation in him.

TOXIC ME

I just want to be held right now.

I want the sheets to consume us, and I want our heartbeats to dance to the same rhythm.

Can you say that you want to see me? Can you say that you need me?

Can you give me a reason to focus on anything but myself?

What if I say please?

Can you answer me?

I DON'T HAVE A CLUE

If I can use a button to silence my mind when my world becomes too chaotic

that will give me some sense of control.

I hate when I am not in control.

When I am not in control, I feel like I am losing a battle.

I strive to be the champion of my life.

I strive to win,

and for me to win, I need to be in control of my habits.

I can't keep living without a sense of purpose.

I can't keep waking up without any direction.

I need to wake up for myself.

I need to be in control of myself.

I can say that so many times, but actually waking up is the hardest part.

Simply getting out of bed is a task in itself.

I'm so close to giving up and I haven't even started.

WOMAN

A woman is a strong opponent against life's trials

She is a resilient blaze of fire, shining brightly over the horizon, illuminating our streets

She is our courage, our rock, our shoulder for when we weep

She is you and she is me, she is in all who conquer adversity

She is a mountain of great heights, she is a road that one does not dare cross

She is the compass that we turn to when we feel lost

She is everything and more

I am a woman and for that I am extraordinary

My strength is exalted in my vulnerability

And my love is expressed through my tears

They tried so many times to tear me down that my resilience invokes fear

HARD TO SWALLOW

I think the comfortability has gotten to me

finding the energy to do tasks is not an easy task

and I jump at any opportunity to obsess over trivial things

the perfectionist in me is scared that I will mess up

so, I don't even try

I'm afraid of failure, so I shy away from progress

I'm choking on my own mistakes and I am lingering away

SOLITUDE IS MY FRIEND

After I wake, I stay in bed a little longer to go back to dreaming.

I've been doing well on my own for two months now, and the thought of someone else has not crossed my mind until now.

But, this time, this thought is not intense, it is not a yearning, nor a cry for a distraction to think of someone else while I ignore my responsibilities.

It is simply a thought, and I only think about a partner when I watch romantic comedies.

I am glad that I have learned how to be alone.

It is quite liberating to be happy and alone.

The crippling feeling of loneliness was once so magnified in my body to the point where it was paralyzing.

Now, it is a distant memory.

I feel as if my heart is slowly piecing together, as I broke it many times.

I also haven't given my body away in several months.

Protecting myself from wicked beings whose sole mission is to destroy anything lovely, is comforting.

And my void is filled by God.

My skin gives off an earthly glow and my spirit is contagious.

And what if somedays I crave the presence of another,

because I know those days will exist.

But, when those days come, I'll sit with myself and ask God to restore my inner balance and she will tell me that I spent years feeling like I need others when I just needed myself.

Solitude is my friend.

ORANGE

The slightest bit of confrontation makes me angry.

Orange simmers in my chest because no one has ever talked to me like that before.

My mom tries with me, I know that she's frustrated.

It was only her who raised me

and sometimes she was too busy working

that she couldn't put me in my place.

My head spins when I make mistakes.

I'm sorry for being a brat

and I'm sorry for being pouty when I don't get my way.

I was raised by a mother who provided me with everything but, a shoulder to cry on.

So, when I'm frustrated I don't know how to express it wisely.

Still having breakdowns because my teenage self doesn't want to die.

Turmoil is ingrained in my DNA and I'm trying hard to fight it off.

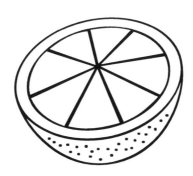

OK, I LIED

I wake up by myself with no one to pull me in closer

to hold me tight from behind and squeeze me

to not let me go without a dozen kisses and hugs

If you thought I was writing this from a place of longing, you're wrong

because I favor my peace and quiet when I wake

and I prefer that no one stops me from seizing my day

I don't let lust blind me from my goals

I enjoy the company of my music and incense when I slumber

I enjoy my tranquility and calm like no other

Ok, I lied

I still want attention

But, I also love my space

Although sometimes I'll allow a lover to put me in a daze

I been thinking about kissing someone all summer

But, I don't see anyone here

interesting enough for a mouth to discover

So, I guess I'm on my own again, finding solace in my inner thoughts

ARCHY

I love when you open your mouth

Because all that comes out of it is passion

You make me want to do better than the bare minimum nonsense that I've been doing

And it doesn't hurt that your South London accent makes my heart quiver

And we can't forget the way your fiery red hair blazes in the sun

And the way your eyes twinkle, more gorgeous than the clearest ocean

And the way your lips press together commandingly when you make a sound

I think today is a better day because I'm contributing to my success

My eyes are weighed down by the heat

And I desperately want my neighbors to notice my new shorts

Besides you, I don't have many other worlds to confine in

It's either you or in my head

WASTING TIME

A cold day in May is like a warm day in March

and I'm sitting on my patio currently wondering where to start

Should I be gentle with myself that I have feared my own power for so long?

Or should I be mad that I threw away countless hours of free time

I'm sitting in a field and the dandelions are welcoming me

They don't ask if they can join me, they just do

They don't second-guess before they act, they charge

in a way that is gentle but firm and there's an army of them

I should compare them to my own resilience

In life, there will be fields that I want to enter in and to succeed, I can't second guess myself

I just have to enter

THIS IS MY SUMMER MEMOIR

and hate runs through my veins

I only love you because of the attention you give me

but, it's time for me to start growing up

I can't keep living in this repressed teenage fantasy all of my life

but, it's so hard

I don't want to grow up honestly

I'm still a child

but, I need to grow up

time is running out and I'm getting tired of my own antics

this is one of those summers where the heat is too humid that it's

not enjoyable to go outside

now I know why all the teenagers come out in the night-time

you seem like the perfect distraction

numbed-out and purposeless

gives us enough time to waste time

I woke up at 8:30 but,

stayed in bed until 12

I'm upset that I turned down that job offer

I got too caught up in the pleasure of the moment

that I wasn't looking to my future

I think that guys can sense when I'm feeling desperate

I often think that I'm too vain

how am I so self-absorbed but still so insecure?

I think I like you for all the wrong reasons

I'm staring at your lips, wishing you would use them more wisely

are they just a device you use for pleasure?

or do they hold substance as well?

I think long hair will always be my weakness

I want to be swept in it

to tell you the truth, I haven't looked at you straight in the face

so, I don't know what I'm getting myself into

I had two slices of bread for breakfast and my fuel tank is

running low

I wish I can smoke again

In fact, I'm thinking of pulling out a spliff right now

but, I don't want my mom to run in on me

and I don't know how my body will react

Is my brain still terrorized by marijuana?

how do you smoke cigarettes but stay away from weed,

saying it's bad for your health?

baby you gon' die in 10 years

and that's not a very long time

considering you're 20 right now

you have all the time in the world

JUNE OPTIMISM

Put your hand into mine

At the beginning of June all I wanted was a summer fling

Bits of fleeting romances and deep make out sessions

Walks in the park and ice cream cones dripping from our hand

But that reality soon turned sour when the little expectations I had were not being met

Until you and I rekindled

and I know you will figure out this is so obviously about you

You're quiet and kind

so quiet that sometimes the air between us feels heavy

I'm figuring out how to stare into your eyes without looking away or making a sound

You're the only person that I walked away from that has been allowed to return back into my life

Usually when I walk away, it's for good

I don't know, this time it's different

between you and I

I'm not in a fragile state of mind anymore

I'm not weighed down by weed smoke and depression

I know I hurt you last time

You're different

and simple

MY INSECURITY IS ACTING UP AGAIN

When I saw you, I should have taken control

and kissed you

I want to be in control

If I'm not in control then I don't feel right

I DON'T KNOW

I love you

I love me

I want my lover to be someone with swagger, with an undoubted coolness, with charm, with charisma, with spark, with passion

a person whose fire lights up under them when they walk

I really don't know much about you

you don't strike me as striking

quiet when you speak

meek

why is your voice so small but at 6'3, you tower over everything?

you're not the person I dreamed of

maybe it's better if it's this way

you're safe, you're kind

you're not dramatic

what is it like to be in love??

I have yet to come close to it

SPIRITUAL BLESSINGS

look at all the work that you're putting in

all the trips to the west end

the early mornings

the full days

and yet you do not realize it

being blinded by men

who don't care about your genuine well-being

baby, get it together

when you get home, pray

and you will be redirected to your divine path

TAKE TIME TO BE SELF-AWARE

Been in and out of my head

My body is aching from the terror around us

The world needs some softness

I have outgrown you and you as well

I have retreated into myself

I keep watch over my heart

JACOB

You make me feel butterflies in my stomach and it leaves me conflicted

A goal of mine was to rise in love but I didn't expect it to be with you

I disappeared for a year

But, surprisingly you waited for me

It leaves me shocked that all this time

You were patiently waiting to embrace me

You're so different than anyone I ever met

Your mouth is silent but your energy is loud

You are content just sitting and staring at me

I pray we find a common ground

I pray I can bring life into you

MOVE ON

you need to learn how to adapt without people

because being with people who don't want to be with you is going to hurt your heart

you already saw how people disappoint you

learn how to adapt without them

what happened to you?

filling your body up with instant gratification will not ease the pain

you're teetering between sadness and frustration

because you think that no one will notice you

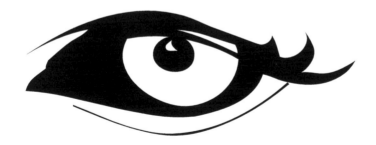

PROGRESSION IS ALL THAT MATTERS

I look at pictures of myself from 3 years ago and see a stranger

I look at pictures of myself from 2 years ago and I barely know her

I look at pictures of myself from last year and we're acquaintances

It's surprising to witness how much I changed

Not only physically but emotionally, mentally and spiritually

I'm glad social media was here for me to document my progression

I may be in the same physical place as I once was

But my mental state is elevated

Now I have the tools to deal with darkness

Now I have the Lord's strength to carry me through

THIS FEELS GOOD

I'm lying in the grass

ants keep crawling up my leg

flies swarm around my head

but, it's still peaceful

I just successfully completed a work out

God, it feels so good to be peaceful

I allow a little heartbreak from time to time

to fuel my creativity

I feel like most artists feel the most inspired when they been through dark times

the kids in my neighborhood ride their bike from early afternoon to sunset

knocking on doors, innocently asking others to play

I'll never return to that state of simplicity

when you grow, your freedom is just as rigid as when you were younger

confined by bills and responsibility

I DON'T KNOW WHAT TO NAME THIS

When I look at you all I think about is pain

and my insecurities creep up from behind me like a shadow in the evening

I knew I should have left you alone

But the stubbornness in me wanted to discover more

Until what I discovered left me feeling like my lungs had no air

I tell myself that I am strong

I tell myself that I will function better if I stop losing my individuality in a lover

But, I am struggling with breaking this pattern

It's difficult to look at your face

You were once so charming, an enigma of mystery

But now all I see is a hollow man

I can see your past in your light brown eyes

and your emotional baggage is reeking

Your goal may be to emotionally manipulate as many girls as you can in one summer

But I won't be a part of it

It's always the cute ones

I STAND ALONE

It's weird to me how a familiar place to someone can be so foreign to another

I'm looking at my landscape and I can't help but quiver in its beauty

Weed smoke surrounds me

and it reminds me of calm

Two lovers who just surpassed puberty walk hand in hand alongside their friends

All wearing floral prints

I'm by myself which is far from unusual

I been riding my bike for an hour

My head completely numb from the music emerging from my earphones

I ventured off into a different neighborhood

It's the same as my neighborhood but different

The youth are less reserved here

There's an air of recklessness and I like it

Laughter fills the streets and veers off into the forest

I've grown to like it here

I seem to forget that I'm one of the few people with melanin here

but, I don't feel alone

I got me

I got nature

I got my music

A LOVE LETTER TO YOU

Trace your fingers between mine

and let me inhale your scent

Tangle me in your hair

and smile so big that your cheeks begin to hurt

Love me up

Love me down

Love me all around

When I saw you, I swear my heart jumped out of my chest

I'm drunken in your embrace

Make me feel like you want me

I only want you

I only see you

JULY REALIZATIONS

It is the start of July and I haven't experienced heart break yet even though it seems like I want to

I admired how you showed me your true colors from the beginning

Saving me a lot of turmoil

You're emotionally unavailable

and I'm emotionally unstable

I understand that there's more to life than cheap thrills and temporary highs

My resilience has been broken down for years

The only coping mechanism I knew was codependency

Until I discovered God

Now I have a sense of self

Now the hurt is not as painful anymore

and the anxiety is not so persistent

Even though I'm 20

I still feel like I'm 17

But I'm working on it...

My goal is to stop coasting through this world

Not everything is fairies and bubbles and rainbows and candy

I need to stop drifting into fantasy land

The real world won't be kind to me

The real world won't wait for my melodramatic episodes to subside

When did I become so derailed?

When did I become so fragile?

Let me pray

I just need to get away

Be alone

I won't take my phone

and I'll calm my mind

REALITY CHECK

I always took pride in being humble

But lately, I have been consumed in my own looks

and I think my ego has overthrown me

Sometimes I catch myself looking in the mirror for a little too long

and I am surprised when I don't receive attention or praise

Reality check

The world does not revolve around me

Ever since my niece was born

I am starting to realize that I have to live a life that is worth admiring

I see how she looks up to me

Everything I do, she's absorbing

I realized how selfish I been

How egotistical I been

How consumed I been with the superficial, shallow pitfalls of the world

I actually like when a man ignores me

Because it makes me realize that dating is not just a hobby

These are real people

that I hit up when I'm feeling bored

Dating is not a game

But I been playing ever since I was 17

When I lost my innocence

REPEATED CYCLE

When I get too caught up in a lover's life

I am reminded that their life is not mine

I can tell myself that this is just for fun

But, if their world becomes my whole world

then it is not fun anymore

It's obsessive

I need to get back to me

Through prayer and meditation

That's where I feel the most exalted

I WANT TO KISS EVERY TATTOO THAT YOU HAVE

I need someone who can inspire me

and I know it's not your fault

No, it's mine

When will I stop waiting for someone to turn my life around

God will

I experienced his love and light

I miss when I was meditating

I miss when I was stretching

Waking up early in the mornings

I want someone to sing a song for me

and love me

like I love myself

I love your eyes

and your nose

and your hair

and your lips

and your tattoos

I want to kiss every tattoo that you have

CALE

Lovers entwined

We're not a good match

I can sense it when we converse

Through awkward laughs

We think about the next thing to say

But, I'm more focused on your face

When you're glancing somewhere else

I'm nervous that you'll catch my gaze

But a part of me also prefers it that way

I always find beauty in the most obscure

I know it's because I see through an idealized lens

Pushing my agenda on my partner because I desperately want them to fulfill my love prototype

that I forget what is right in front of my eyes

When you invite me into your room,

I am enclosed with intimate energy

My body craves that

I don't want to leave

Please put your hand on mine

and I promise I won't be uncomfortable

DRINKING AND THINKING OF YOU DON'T MIX

Please take me

I'm practically begging you at this point

No more passive aggressiveness

I know I deleted your number but I wrote it down somewhere in my room so I can come back to it

I'm calling you now

I'm telling you that I want you

I want you now

Stop playing indifferent

Put your pride aside for just a moment

I already left mine at the door

I'm coming inside now

and I sit on the edge of the bed

playing naive to what is about to happen

But I just want to be held

Just tell me you want me

In fact, tell me you love me

From the deepest darkest depths of my heart I want to be loved romantically

and you're the perfect prototype

Can you tell that I'm talking about you?

Can you tell that you're on my mind?

Can you tell that this poem is for you?

Can you tell that I want you?

Can you tell that I like you?

Can you tell that I lowered my standards for you?

I know I'm better than this

But it's kind of fun to be foolish

I left you a thousand love letters and 2 voicemails since last Friday and you have yet to answer

What are you even doing that's taking up all your time?

Who are you seeing?

Who are you giving all your attention to?

I should be on your mind when you wake up

I should be on your mind when you're at work

When you're in the shower

When you're eating cereal with too much milk

Why can't you call me?

Is our romance only limited to text messages and the occasional link up every 3 weeks?

I'm practically screaming out your name right now

Don't leave me hanging

WE ALL MOVE ON

It's weird when the roles are reversed

I used to be the one hurting

and grieving over a love that never came to blossom

a young girl, so naïve to the tricks and implications of love

but, I soon became the heartbreaker

and I see how you're hurting

and I know why you're ignoring me

I should just leave you alone

I came to understand that I have manipulating tendencies

I'm not perfect

I'm sorry

I'm better at being a friend

Please don't like me, you don't want this problem

I see you and

I know you're hurting

I'm sorry

I'm not perfect

I'm better at being a friend

Please don't like me, you don't want this problem

YOU ARE A DIVINE CREATION

Pouring my hopes and dreams into this cup

Our romance is like the sunset, lovely but quick to fade

These days my phone stays on do not disturb

I remember when I used to entertain
5 people at once

But that euphoria you get from cheap
attention quickly dies

and you're back at square one, feeling
hollow again

Feeling all the hurt you tried so hard
to ignore

and this time the sting is more painful

Your chest tightens, restricting your
air flow and your stomach churns

Is it really worth it to put yourself
through this stress?

Look in the mirror and tell me what
you see

I know you see a person who is broken

I know you see a person who feels like
they can't survive without breathing
in a lover's air

But, I'll tell you that you'll breathe so much better when you have your
own air

Do me a favor and be good to yourself

Wake up early

Eat breakfast

Exercise

Ask God to supply your needs

Those empty feelings will subside

The anxiety will fade away

Don't put all your identity into another person, my love

You are a divine creation

Printed in the United States
By Bookmasters